TROPE

ICONIC ARTISTS

A Celebration of the World's Extraordinary Artists

Illustrated by
DAVID LEE CSICSKO

Text by
**DAVID LEE CSICSKO
& LINDY SINCLAIR**

CONTENTS	PAGE
Foreword Tom Bachtell	4
Introduction Megha Ralapati	6
Henri de Toulouse-Lautrec 1864-1901	11
Suzanne Valadon 1865-1938	12
Henri Matisse 1869-1954	15
Alice Bailly 1872-1938	17
Piet Mondrian 1872-1944	18
Paul Klee 1879-1940	21
Pablo Picasso 1881-1973	23
Amedeo Modigliani 1884-1920	24
Robert & Sonia Delaunay R: 1885-1941 S: 1885-1979	27
Tarsila do Amaral 1886-1973	28
Tsuguharu Foujita 1886-1968	31
Diego Rivera & Frida Kahlo D: 1886-1957 F: 1907-1954	33
Marcel Duchamp 1887-1968	35
Georgia O'Keeffe 1887-1986	37
Sophie Taeuber-Arp 1889-1943	39
Lyubov Popova 1889-1924	40
Egon Schiele 1890-1918	43
Archibald Motley 1891-1981	44
Fortunato Depero 1892-1960	46
Henry Darger 1892-1973	48
Pauline Simon 1894-1976	51
Tamara de Lempicka 1898-1980	52
Alexander Calder 1898-1976	54
René Magritte 1898-1967	57
Louise Nevelson 1899-1988	59

ICONIC ARTISTS

William Henry Johnson 1901-1970	**61**
Wifredo Lam 1902-1982	**63**
Joseph Cornell 1903-1972	**65**
Salvador Dalí 1904-1989	**67**
Loïs Mailou Jones 1905-1998	**69**
Lee Godie 1908-1994	**70**
Lee Krasner & Jackson Pollock L: 1908-1984 J: 1912-1956	**72**
Remedios Varo 1908-1963	**75**
Gertrude Abercrombie 1909-1977	**76**
Corita Kent 1918-1986	**78**
Ruth Asawa 1926-2013	**80**
Andy Warhol 1928-1987	**82**
Marisol Escobar 1930-2016	**85**
Baya Mahieddine 1931-1998	**86**
Nam June Paik 1932-2006	**88**
Ed Paschke 1939-2004	**90**
ORLAN 1947-	**92**
Mr. Imagination 1948-2012	**95**
David McDermott & Peter McGough D: 1952- P: 1958-	**97**
Keith Haring 1958-1990	**99**
Nick Cave 1959-	**101**
Jean-Michel Basquiat 1960-1988	**103**
Mickalene Thomas 1971-	**104**
Bisa Butler 1973-	**106**
Salman Toor 1983-	**108**
About the Authors	**111**

FOREWORD

TOM BACHTELL

Acclaimed artist, illustrator, and caricaturist

The book you are holding is a David Lee Csicsko treasury and field guide to fifty significant and fascinating artists of the past 150 years. In it, Csicsko portrays and collects lore about his subjects, from the French Henri de Toulouse-Lautrec and Suzanne Valadon to the queer-forward Salman Toor (who references absinthe—Lautrec's favorite spirit—in the green glow of his paintings); from the schooled to the self-taught; from the familiar to the hard-to-categorize; from the celebrated to the unjustly neglected. Paul Klee, Pauline Simon, Mr. Imagination, Corita Kent, Baya Mahieddine, Keith Haring, Mickalene Thomas, Pablo Picasso, Nick Cave, and Henry Darger are just a few represented here. Some of these names are likely quite familiar; others may be new to you.

    David Lee Csicsko is himself a prolific and singular artist, but he frequently reminds me that he is also "a visual detective." Whether David is exploring a faraway city, or dropping in to a museum or gallery, or browsing a bookstore, or walking his dachshund in his neighborhood, he constantly and fearlessly takes photographs, makes sketches, and collects stories. He shares both his art and his discoveries any way that he can (he has been known to approach people he perceives to be out-of-town visitors to Chicago and give them personal tours of the Art Institute)—most often these days on social media, and now in this beautiful book, always with a generous accompaniment of insights and observations.

In Csicsko and co-author Lindy Sinclair's telling, many of the artists here are connected through friendship and that is an important part of the story of art. Toulouse-Lautrec, for example, encouraged his model and lover Suzanne Valadon to pursue drawing and painting and introduced her to Edgar Degas, who became her painting adviser and teacher. Artists often work alone, but they are hardly lonely figures. One artist meeting another is an electric and galvanizing event—the artist just met becomes fixed in the other's consciousness as a mutual witness and observer and interpreter and mirror of human experience, a fellow cultural antenna and neuron. Whether an artist is academically trained or self-taught doesn't matter. In this way, artists form a community with other artists—by turns appreciative, supportive, collaborative, inspiring, sometimes competitive, even argumentative. We learn and grow; we are what we are because of each other.

In my own friendship with David Lee Csicsko, we have been influencing and learning from one another for almost fifty years. Though we have both made a living through art, David is schooled in art, and I am schooled in music, English, and dance. I met this remarkable man when he threw a picnic in his college dorm room in Cleveland—he had spread a bounty of treats and delicacies from Cleveland's West Side Market on a blanket on the drab linoleum floor for everyone entering the room to partake in. "Isn't it WONDERFUL?" was his command to us to join the picnic. David and I have since shared studio space, traveled together, gone to concerts and lectures and plays, told stories, experienced laughter, joy, and sadness, and generally witnessed the world as friends and artists. David tells the story that we met the artist Lee Godie together when we stopped to talk to her one day as she somewhat irascibly and surreptitiously displayed her artwork in front of Chicago's Wrigley Building. She was relatively sociable that day, believe it or not, and not only described her habit of lodging a wheel of cheese and cheese knife in her blouse for snacking on visits to the Art Institute, but also freely critiqued my own work when I showed it to her ("I draw beauty. Your work is homely."). A rich artistic experience, indeed.

Just as David continues to explore and behold and create and share with an "Isn't this WONDERFUL?" to everyone in his vicinity, so has he informed the artists' portraits and biographies in this book. Through his unique artistic prism, he has created a wonderful and wide-ranging treasury for you. It is meant to be savored and shared. Enjoy.

INTRODUCTION

MEGHA RALAPATI

Art curator and writer

One of the best things about growing up in Chicago was the visits I made with my family or on class trips to the Art Institute. The building seemed like the most magnificent and grand, yet somehow cozy and intimate home I could imagine. I wanted to live there. Walking up the majestic stairs off Michigan Avenue, the lions would greet me, and I would step into the cool, calm of the entryway. As a young person, the artworks I was most drawn to were some of the museum's greatest hits. When looking at *Paris Street; Rainy Day* by Gustave Caillebotte, one of my favorite painters, I could feel the wet cobblestones underfoot and smell the fresh rain while hearing the hurried click of women's shoes. It was here in the Asian galleries that I encountered an exquisite granite sculpture of the Buddha sitting peacefully, inviting us to share in his meditative state. Swimming between artistic styles and periods, geographic regions and appearances, I wondered how one place could house such vastly distinct things. What could they possibly share? Despite their differences, they all had one thing in common: they were created by an artist.

Many people value artists because they make things, which in special cases like these can transcend time and place, long outliving the maker. Yes, the ceiling of the Sistine Chapel receives millions of visitors every year and Michelangelo is long gone. We don't even know the names of the Edo artists who made the Benin bronzes, but these statues were stolen from Africa over a hundred years ago and are only now being returned.

What truly makes artists important, however, is less what they create and more so how they think. To create art, something wholly new that may not serve any instrumental function, both requires and refines a capacity to view the world beyond what it currently is. As humans, we've established our systems, and roads, our infrastructures, and laws. We've created rules that claim to govern society, circumscribing how people should behave, live, believe, love, parent, learn, fight, and consume. But it's artists who remind us that these are merely illusions. They're hyperrealistic mirages that can fool us into thinking they're real, when, in fact, other worlds are entirely possible.

Artists are trained to see beyond the here and now and to engage deeply in the practice of creating new possibilities. Through their work, they demonstrate new possibilities for how we might live in the present. Their efforts over time, what we might call a "creative practice," are punctuated by moments of form, what we might call "artworks," which can move us as viewers out of the realm of the cerebral, and often more deeply into our bodies. In an encounter with art, we sometimes forget time and place. Put another way, we remember that "clock time" as described by philosopher Eckhart Tolle, which shapes how we experience most of our days, is just an invention. When moved by an artwork, we feel somehow linked to the maker and to each other, a quiet reminder of our deep interconnectedness with all things. In a moment like this, it's possible to even lose our identifications—with our nation, our gender, our social class. We're reminded that these too were never real, despite their very real impact on our lives.

The artists in this book represent a scintillatingly dynamic, wide-ranging group from the most highly lauded, the academically trained, the self-taught, the mainstay of the Western canon, to the most courageous, nonconforming artists of today. Not everyone needs to become an artist, but our world would surely benefit if we all, in our own domains, practiced thinking like one.

ACKNOWLEDGEMENTS

Iconic Artists is a bright, enthusiastic look at fifty artists from Henri de Toulouse-Lautrec to artists living and working today. As an "art kid" who entered poster contests all the time, Toulouse-Lautrec was my "art guy," the artist who made the poster into an art form. It was important to me that I begin this book with the artist who has meant so much to me throughout my life. I fully believe that to embrace contemporary art, we should look also into the past, and celebrate these visionary rule breakers.

Here's to the people who encouraged me on my crazy wonderful artistic path: my family, friends, and teachers, notably Anthony Waring (Morton Senior High School) and Robert Jergens (Cleveland Institute of Art). In art school, I made many lifelong friends, including Carol Falcone Chiantis, Lori Bolt, Birdie Thaler, Tom Bachtell, Andrew McEachern, Michael Reardon, Sharon Connelly Conklin, Caroline Burton and Catherine Butler. Here's to my favorite people to talk about art with: Lorin Adolph, Steve Musgrave, Sharon Evans, Peter Emmerich, Jens Hanke, Ulrike Dornis, and Sean Karemmaker. A special thank you to David Syrek, Christine Benoodt, and Patrick Bade. Here's to Deirdre Daw, a friend and great artist we lost too soon.

DAVID LEE CSICSKO

With love and thanks to my favorite musician and my favorite future author-illustrator, my own in-house art committee. And for everyone, in any artistic or craft field, who creates just because they need to. Don't let anyone make you feel like your work doesn't make you an artist—the time, care, and attention it takes to make anything new proves them wrong.

LINDY SINCLAIR

ICONIC ARTISTS

HENRI de TOULOUSE-LAUTREC

1864 – 1901

ALBI (FRANCE)

ICONIC ARTISTS

HENRI DE TOULOUSE-LAUTREC

Chronicler of Paris nightlife who turned commercial posters into fine art

Henri de Toulouse-Lautrec stood less than five feet tall but is a giant of art history. He was the first artist to turn advertising into fine art, breaking down the definitions of high and low. His posters captured the spirit of Paris nightlife in the late 19th century, an artistic time capsule of urban life.

Toulouse-Lautrec came from an aristocratic family. He loved horses, but weak bones and a couple of falls that didn't heal properly kept him from riding and affected his growth. He turned to art instead and convinced his parents to send him to Paris to study, where he became lifelong friends with Vincent Van Gogh, a fellow student.

The young artist went wild for the city's cafés, cabarets, and theaters—the first "club kid" artist. He felt at home with the circus performers and dancers, people pushed to society's margins. Charming and funny, he was the life of the party, but he could use his small size to fade into the background when he wanted to observe and sketch. He painted his subjects in a very human way, showing the emotion behind the glamour and makeup. An exceptional draftsman, Toulouse-Lautrec gave a delicate hand-drawn quality to all his work; even his paintings look as if they were drawn with a paintbrush rather than a pencil.

Inspired by Japanese woodblock prints, Toulouse-Lautrec experimented with color lithography, a new type of printmaking. His first advertising poster for the Moulin Rouge nightclub made him an overnight success. His images made showgirls into superstars. He understood how to catch the eye, and his posters are considered foundations of graphic design.

Toulouse-Lautrec died at 36 years old, in poor health from his excessive drinking. It was a tragically young end for an artist whose work is one of the pillars of modern art. He was a profound influence on a young Pablo Picasso. Without Toulouse-Lautrec raising commercial art to the level of fine art, Andy Warhol and pop art may not have been possible decades later. While his drawings, prints, and paintings depict Paris's Belle Époque era, his innovations continue to echo through time.

ICONIC ARTISTS

SUZANNE VALADON

Model turned painter who transformed the way women were represented in art

Suzanne Valadon (born Marie-Clémentine) grew up on the streets of Montmartre, the bohemian neighborhood of Paris where writers and artists defied society's rules and made up their own. It should be no surprise that this independent, energetic woman refused to accept fine art as a man's world, forging her own path as an artist and changing the way women were portrayed.

Valadon was born to a single mother, taking odd jobs before she was even a teenager. She had always loved drawing but couldn't afford art lessons, so she began modeling for artists to observe and learn from them. Her beauty and fun-loving personality made her popular with some of the era's most important painters, including Pierre-Auguste Renoir.

She had a romantic relationship with Henri de Toulouse-Lautrec, who not only painted her but encouraged and financially supported her (and who suggested the name Suzanne). Already well-known himself, Toulouse-Lautrec was so impressed by her drawing that he introduced her to master painter Edgar Degas. Degas became a close friend and helped her get noticed by art dealers.

Valadon's talent spoke for itself, and she became the first woman with work admitted to the Société Nationale des Beaux-Arts. She had a bold, unromantic style, painting women in a matter-of-fact way, imperfections and all. She always kept her rebellious streak: *Adam and Eve* is possibly the first male nude to be exhibited by a woman, and it was modeled after herself and her much younger boyfriend.

Valadon spent her life surrounded by other artists. Her son, Maurice Utrello, also became a well-known painter and was close friends with Amedeo Modigliani. When she died, Pablo Picasso attended her funeral. "I paint with the stubbornness I need for living," she once said, "and I've found that all painters who love their art do the same."

SUZANNE VALADON

1865 – 1938

BESSINES-SUR-GARTEMPE (FRANCE)

HENRI MATISSE

1869 – 1954

LE CATEAU-CAMBRÉSIS (FRANCE)

HENRI MATISSE

A gentle giant of innovation who changed the course of modern art

As a young law clerk, Henri Matisse had done a little drawing, but began painting while recovering from appendicitis. He loved it so much that he quit his budding law career to study art in Paris. Modern art might look very different today if he had just gotten better and gone back to work—Matisse became one of the most revolutionary artists of the 20th century.

As a student, Matisse was drawn to the impressionist paintings of Paul Cézanne and Vincent Van Gogh. He changed the way he applied paint, playing with pointillism and using more lively colors. A trip to the south of France, with its bright Mediterranean sunlight, was the creative oxygen that set his palette on fire. Matisse turned to bold brush strokes and vibrant colors that made even landscapes look shocking, a style dubbed fauvism (from the French for "wild beast," as he was called by one grumpy art critic).

Along with his wild colors, Matisse flattened and abstracted his images, creating a whole new visual language. Flowing lines and bold colors expressed feelings about the natural world instead of depicting it. He created and curated a painted world that was beautiful and alive, constantly moving towards simplification.

A notorious workaholic, Matisse produced thousands of paintings, drawings, sculptures, and prints over his lifetime. When his health declined and he could no longer stand, he worked from his bed or a wheelchair with the help of assistants, adapting his forms and techniques in new and inventive ways. He cut shapes from hand-painted pieces of paper, a method he used to design stained glass windows and create book illustrations.

Together with his friend and rival Pablo Picasso, Matisse changed modern art forever. Artists from Mark Rothko to Keith Haring have been influenced by Matisse's balanced shapes, playful colors, or innovative techniques. Blockbuster exhibits of his work prove that his genius still moves and excites us today.

ALICE BAILLY

1872 - 1938

GENEVA (SWITZERLAND)

ICONIC ARTISTS

ALICE BAILLY

Swiss avant-garde painter and textile artist who was an early pioneer of mixed media

Alice Bailly grew up with a love of culture and learning, but she didn't seriously start pursuing art until she was in her 30s. She made up for lost time, applying her talent to many different art styles but always making them her own.

Bailly moved to Paris and started out exhibiting wood engravings, but the bold brushstrokes and vibrant colors of the new fauvism movement caught her eye. Bailly embraced this freedom of form and color that valued emotional expression over realism and began applying it to her own work.

In Paris, Bailly befriended Juan Gris, Francis Picabia, Marie Laurencin, and other avant-garde modernist painters who influenced her work and her later life. She explored many new styles, developing her own interpretations of cubism, futurism, and Dadaism. In 1912, her work was chosen to represent Switzerland in a traveling exhibit seen across Europe.

Bailly had to return to Geneva at the start of World War I. There she invented her "wool paintings," mixed-media creations that used strands of vividly colored yarn to imitate brushstrokes. She sometimes added paper collage and painted elements, and the combination made many artists realize that fine art did not have to be limited to canvas and brush. For Bailly, there was no difference between her oil paintings and her wool creations; she was simply using new tools to increase the number of ways she could express herself.

ICONIC ARTISTS

PIET MONDRIAN

Abstract pioneer who stripped art down to its most basic elements

To see Piet Mondrian's early landscapes of the Dutch countryside, you'd never guess he would become famous for stark, minimalist paintings of crisp black lines and blocks of primary colors. Mondrian was a trailblazer in abstract painting, essentially inventing an entirely new art form based on stripping everything down to its absolute essence.

Like many artists, Mondrian started out painting realistic scenes. He was especially fascinated by trees. Over time, he started to see the negative space between branches rather than the tree itself. Upon moving to Paris, he was exposed to more modern art. Cubist paintings by Pablo Picasso and Georges Braque inspired him to change his painting style and limit the number of colors he used.

Mondrian began creating very pared-down paintings, blocks of red, blue, and yellow framed by sharp black lines that he would spend weeks perfecting—no rulers allowed. He continually simplified, trying to capture what he saw as the "pure," universal order hidden by the visible world. The way he broke art down to its most fundamental elements changed and shaped modern art. It was the desire to make these bold, geometric elements move that later motivated Alexander Calder to invent the mobile.

In contrast with the strict minimalism of his paintings, Mondrian loved jazz music and the buzz and activity of his adopted home of New York. With *Broadway Boogie Woogie*, Mondrian's last finished painting, he broke his own rules: no black lines, no solid bars of color. Instead, little blocks of color parade across the canvas like city intersections. That a painting made of such simple pieces can capture so much rhythm and movement is the ultimate proof of Mondrian's mastery.

PIET MONDRIAN

1872 – 1944

AMERSFOORT (NETHERLANDS)

PAUL KLEE

1879 – 1940

MÜNCHENBUCHSEE (SWITZERLAND)

ICONIC ARTISTS

PAUL KLEE

Playful and witty innovator of abstract art and color theory

German Swiss artist Paul Klee was born into a family of musicians and was himself a talented violinist. His lifelong love of music and interest in the subconscious mind helped him create a groundbreaking style that has been inspiring artists ever since.

At first, Klee concentrated mostly on black-and-white drawings or prints. Then he met Wassily Kandinsky, a pioneer of abstract art. The Blue Rider, Kandinsky's group of artists, believed that art could express spiritual truths through line and color—a radical change from using art to mirror the visual world. Kandinsky and Klee became lifelong friends and influences on each other's work.

In 1914, a trip to Tunisia ignited Klee's sense of color. His work became more abstract, using almost childlike shapes and mixing in symbols, simple stick figures, and imaginative references to music and literature. Klee described drawing as "a line going for a walk," and his paintings are full of movement and playfulness. He often practiced his violin before painting, and he borrowed ideas from music theory to combine colored blocks as if they were musical chords.

From 1921 to 1931, Klee taught at the Bauhaus, a German school combining crafts with fine art. He thought deeply about color and design theory, and his collection of lectures and essays are considered as important to understanding modern art as Leonardo da Vinci's writings were for the Renaissance.

Klee's unique work drew strong reactions. His sense of spontaneity and magic appealed to the surrealists, who thought his paintings reflected the way dreams combine random elements. When the Nazis took over Germany, they declared his art "degenerate," or harmful to society. In the end, though, Klee's poetic visual language and ideas about color are still valued and appreciated today.

PABLO PICASSO

1881 - 1973

MÁLAGA (SPAIN)

ICONIC ARTISTS

PABLO PICASSO

The wild man of 20th century art who threw out the rulebook and changed art forever

Pablo Picasso was an unstoppable force of creativity, working until the day he died at 91 years old. He pioneered cubism and artistic collage. He was a painter, sculptor, printmaker, ceramicist, theater designer, and writer who influenced 20th century art more than anyone else.

Picasso was born to be an artist; his father was a painter, and his mother claimed his first word was "piz," short for the Spanish word for pencil. He began formal study very early but was experimenting with styles of his own by his late teens, inspired by Henri de Toulouse-Lautrec, Edgar Degas, and El Greco. After the death of a friend, he spent several years in his Blue Period, painting in a melancholy, blue-tinted style, followed by a pink-tinted Rose Period as he settled permanently in Paris.

The painter's style—and all of modern art—was about to change forever. Picasso was infatuated with the Iberian and African tribal art he saw in Paris museums. He studied their sharp geometry and flat planes and incorporated them into new paintings that were shocking even to his friends. Working together with painter Georges Braque, they created cubism, where multiple perspectives are shown at the same time by breaking them into pieces and rearranging them. It was an entirely new visual language that abandoned rules used in fine art for hundreds of years. The idea that art did not need to copy nature was an earthquake that changed the face of European art.

Picasso's curiosity and versatility led him to design ballet sets, experiment with surrealism, and create welded metal sculptures. He splashed his emotions on canvas, from his volatile personal relationships to the righteous outrage of *Guernica*, his powerful masterpiece about the horror and destruction of war. He revisited the Old Masters of his native Spain, painting his own versions of their works. For almost 80 years, Pablo Picasso explored an eclectic range of styles, subjects, and media, becoming a living legend.

ICONIC ARTISTS

AMEDEO MODIGLIANI

Starving-artist legend who brought together the Italian Renaissance and modern art

Amedeo Modigliani was the heartthrob of bohemian Paris, the charming Italian Jewish artist who spouted poetry from memory and favored bright neck scarves. He wanted to be a painter since he was a child and studied classical painting and sculpture in Italy, but moved to Paris in 1906 for its exciting modern art scene. He quickly became friends with Pablo Picasso, Chaïm Soutine, and other well-known artists and writers.

Modigliani admired Paul Cézanne and Henri de Toulouse-Lautrec, but he struggled to find his own style until he met Constantin Brâncuși. Brâncuși, like many other Parisian artists at the time, was borrowing heavily from African tribal art, seeking out African masks and folk art arriving from faraway French colonies. Modigliani loved Brâncuși's strong, simplified forms, and began making his own mask-like sculptures, large human heads stretched like taffy with tiny mouths and long, thin noses. The figures in his paintings also took on this stretched-out quality, with long necks and oval faces that often did not have the eyes filled in.

His work was popular among other artists, but Modigliani didn't see much success during his lifetime. A landlord who took paintings when Modigliani couldn't pay his rent used the canvases to patch old mattresses. His friends called him "Modi," a play on the French word for "cursed." He was finally starting to get noticed in 1919, when his work was one of the stars of a major exhibition in London. Unfortunately, after many years of poor health and bad habits, Modigliani died just a few months later.

Modigliani's work didn't fit into a specific art movement but was a sort of bridge between classical Italian painting and a new modernism. His spare lines and stylized faces still capture so much emotion, and his style is now instantly recognizable to art lovers around the world.

AMEDEO MODIGLIANI

1884 – 1920

LIVORNO (ITALY)

SONIA & ROBERT DELAUNAY

Power couple of avant-garde Paris

Robert and Sonia Delaunay were soulmates, in life and in art. They met and married in Paris, the center of a creative explosion at the beginning of the 20th century. Their social circle included Marc Chagall, Wassily Kandinsky, Diego Rivera, and many more of the era's most influential artists. The Delaunays were the power couple of the avant-garde, together creating a brilliant body of work while each maintaining their own artistic identities.

Both experimented with the fragmented style of cubism, but where Pablo Picasso and Georges Braque used more muted colors, the Delaunays employed bolder, more intense colors with dynamic movement. They believed that color could be used like musical notes, combining to create harmony. This style of strong color and geometric shapes became known as Orphism. They were enchanted by the creative spirit and modernism of Paris itself and used the Eiffel Tower as a muse and symbol in many of their artistic projects.

In addition to painting, Robert was a theorist (he wrote a major book about using color to represent light) and a champion of all things new. Sonia went beyond painting into textiles, theater costumes, and housewares, mixing the Russian folk crafts of her heritage with modern abstract forms to create delightful living art. She was wildly successful as a fashion designer, supporting the family even when war brought hard times. She continued making great work after Robert's death and was the first living female artist to have a retrospective exhibit at the Louvre in 1964.

Robert and Sonia were each other's biggest fans and greatest champions. They were a meeting of the minds, collaborating as equals while each producing deeply creative, innovative work of their own.

ICONIC ARTISTS

TARSILA DO AMARAL

Brazil's queen mother of modern art

When Tarsila do Amaral left Brazil to study art in Paris, she wrote in a letter home that her goal was "to be the painter of my country." She became one of Brazil's best-known and most-loved artists, borrowing from European avant-garde ideas to create new visual icons for a rapidly changing country.

Most daughters of wealthy Brazilian families at that time were not well-educated, but do Amaral's family encouraged her studies in Barcelona and Paris. She studied at the Académie Julian, a famous school for modern art, where she met Pablo Picasso and was taught by Fernand Léger. Many of the early cubists were inspired by African masks, and do Amaral was reminded of all the different cultures of her home, where non-European influences were strong but often ignored.

She came home and traveled the country, seeking inspiration in the landscapes, people, and folk traditions. She combined European modernist ideas with Brazilian subjects to create a bold, sensual visual language that was very new to the conservative Brazilian art world. Her unique vision is a world of orange and lemon sliced suns over rounded, almost cartoon-like abstract figures, a multicultural Brazil both festive and melancholy.

Do Amaral was part of the Grupo dos Cinco, or Group of Five, who rejected traditional rules in favor of experimentation. They called themselves "intellectual surrealist cannibals" who devoured avant-garde ideas to create something new and uniquely Brazilian. Their work established São Paulo as a new center for the arts and inspired a new generation of South American artists to explore and create.

TARSILA DO AMARAL

1886 – 1973

SÃO PAULO (BRAZIL)

TSUGUHARU FOUJITA

1886 - 1968

TOKYO (JAPAN)

TSUGUHARU FOUJITA

Icon of Jazz Age Paris for his groundbreaking mix of European and Japanese styles

Tsuguharu Foujita always wanted to be an artist: he won prizes in school, sold a painting to the emperor of Japan, and was asked to paint the emperor of Korea. But Foujita had his sights set on Paris, the center of the avant-garde art world—when he moved there in 1913, he wrote a letter home telling his father to "consider me dead until I become famous."

It didn't take long. Foujita took Jazz Age Paris by storm. He quickly became friends with Pablo Picasso, Henri Matisse, Amedeo Modigliani, and other prominent artists. He changed his last name from "Fujita" to "Foujita" to sound more French. He had the glamorous, flamboyant style of a 1920s Andy Warhol: his big gold earrings, bold tortoiseshell glasses, and sharp bowl haircut were later copied on shop window mannequins as his fame grew.

Japanese objects and art were all the rage, and Foujita had near-instant success by carefully combining elements of European and Japanese art. He painted typically "western" subjects like self-portraits and female nudes (plus lots of cats), but with delicate, precise lines drawn from traditional Japanese painting. He used ultra-thin Japanese menso brushes and added touches of sumi ink. He created a special glaze that gave his paintings an unusual, pearly glow.

Foujita threw lavish parties but didn't pay his taxes and fled to Latin America in the early 1930s. World War II brought him back to Japan, where he created propaganda art for the imperial army that still makes him controversial among art historians. Permanently returning to France after the war, Foujita eventually became a French citizen and added "Léonard" to his name, a tribute to Leonardo da Vinci. He converted to Catholicism and spent his later years focused on religious themes, including painting frescoes for a chapel.

DIEGO RIVERA

1886 – 1957

GUANAJUATO (MEXICO)

FRIDA KAHLO

1907 – 1954

MEXICO CITY (MEXICO)

ICONIC ARTISTS

DIEGO RIVERA & FRIDA KAHLO

The dynamic duo who created uniquely Mexican modern art

Diego Rivera was already an international art celebrity when he met Frida Kahlo. He had spent years in Paris, exploring cubism and mingling with Pablo Picasso, Amedeo Modigliani, and the rest of the Paris art set. Back in Mexico, he simplified his style to revive the ancient mural traditions of the Mayans with bold, breathtaking public frescoes that illustrated Mexico's history and culture and made him a national hero.

Rivera was a physically large man with a larger-than-life personality, but he met his match in Kahlo, a small woman 20 years younger and in fragile health. For the next 25 years, these two colorful characters orbited around each other in a tumultuous relationship full of drama and passion.

In some ways, Rivera and Kahlo were total opposites. He painted on a grand scale, while her paintings were mostly very small, since she often had to work from her bed. Rivera covered walls with epic scenes of history and national identity; Kahlo told dark fairy tales of magic and pain, many of them surreal self-portraits. But together, they formed the center of a new Mexican avant-garde, both devoted to building a modernism firmly rooted in Mexican traditions and identities apart from European influence.

Both artists were deeply influential in their own ways. Rivera's electrifying murals captured the imagination of his country with their intensity and powerful storytelling. Kahlo's work, often personal stories full of symbols and mystery, broke new ground for emotional expression. While Kahlo was overshadowed by Rivera for most of her life, she has become a feminist and LGBTQ+ icon and is now considered one of Mexico's most important modern artists. While Rivera's impressive career is still celebrated, it is now Kahlo who is the international superstar.

MARCEL DUCHAMP

1887 – 1968

BLAINVILLE-CREVON (FRANCE)

ICONIC ARTISTS

MARCEL DUCHAMP

Father of conceptual art who erased the boundaries between works of art and everyday objects

Marcel Duchamp was described by fellow painter Willem de Kooning as a "one-man movement." With playfulness and a sharp intellect, Duchamp redefined art for the 20th century. He turned the role of the artist inside-out, from someone creating objects of beauty to a maverick bound to question and subvert the "normal" way of doing things.

Duchamp started painting as a teenager and tried out different styles, but he quickly grew bored emulating painters from the past. The world was changing quickly around him, and he wanted to experiment with new ideas. He rejected the notion that art was just beautiful paintings; he wanted his art to make people think.

Duchamp saw beauty in everyday objects, and thought that since paint itself was industrially made, why not make art out of other manufactured items? He presented a bicycle wheel, a snow shovel, even a urinal as sculpture. He took a postcard of Leonardo da Vinci's beloved *Mona Lisa*, considered the greatest painting in Western art and an ideal of feminine beauty, and added a beard and mustache. His "readymades," as he called them, stopped the art world in its tracks. With humor and irony, Duchamp attacked highbrow rules and suggested that art was whatever an artist decided it was.

In addition to art, Duchamp was famously obsessed with chess, sometimes directing life-size lawn games with people in costume as pieces. He designed his own chess set, and in 1923 declared that his art career was over and he was devoting the rest of his life to chess (though he didn't stay away from art forever).

Duchamp was associated with cubism, Dadaism, and surrealism, but his influence was much larger than a specific movement. Later artists like Andy Warhol and even Banksy have used Duchamp's ideas to question how we engage with art and popular culture. He was a thinker, a disrupter, and a radical who opened the door to entirely new worlds of what art could be and what artists could do.

GEORGIA O'KEEFFE

1887 – 1986

SUN PRAIRIE, WISCONSIN (USA)

GEORGIA O'KEEFFE

The earth mother of modern art

Georgia O'Keeffe made many stops on her journey to becoming one of America's most famous artists. Born into a family that valued both art and education, she studied at the School of the Art Institute of Chicago and the Art Students League in New York. While her classes were more traditional, she often went to exhibits at Gallery 291, one of the few places in the US showing European avant-garde artists like Henri Matisse.

O'Keeffe moved around for several years, eventually teaching art in South Carolina. She experimented with interesting, abstract drawings of natural forms and mailed one to an old art school classmate, who showed it to the owner of Gallery 291, photographer Alfred Stieglitz. He was so impressed that he put on her first solo art show and then offered to support her for a year if she moved back to New York to focus on art. O'Keeffe and Stieglitz eventually married and were at the center of a group of artists and photographers trying to adapt modernist ideas to a uniquely American perspective.

By the 1920s, O'Keeffe was already becoming known as one of the country's most important painters. She never followed the trends of modern art, always staying true to her own vision of nature's most essential, abstract forms. Her subjects were mostly landscapes, flowers, and bones, which she often painted over and over with different nuances of color or shape.

She fell in love with New Mexico's desert landscape in 1929 and returned every summer, relocating permanently in 1949. She traveled the world but always returned to paint the sun-bleached skulls, glorious flowers, and majestic mountains of rural New Mexico. She has become a feminist icon for her achievements and an artistic icon for the bold vision of her work.

SOPHIE TAEUBER-ARP

1889 – 1943

DAVOS (SWITZERLAND)

ICONIC ARTISTS

SOPHIE TAEUBER-ARP

Multitalented artist and designer at the center of the Dada movement

Sophie Taeuber-Arp was the very definition of a multidisciplinary artist. It seems like there's nothing she didn't do! She was a painter, sculptor, textile designer, costume designer, furniture and interior designer, architect, dancer, teacher, magazine editor, and more. Like the Bauhaus school, she believed there should be no separation between fine art and good design. Her work combined traditional crafts with abstract modernism, bringing art into everyday life in the hopes of creating a more beautiful world.

Along with her husband and frequent collaborator, sculptor and painter Jean Arp, Taeuber-Arp was a key member of Dada, an artistic movement that arose in Zurich as a reaction to the horrors of World War I. Dada art, literature, and performances were playful, even nonsensical, often spontaneous, and strongly against materialism and nationalism. They were the punk art kids of their day. Her wide circle of friends included many influential artists, such as Sonia and Robert Delaunay, Marcel Duchamp, Alexander Calder, and Wassily Kandinsky.

Taeuber-Arp had a distinctive style with geometric shapes and lines that still felt rhythmic and beautiful. In 1918, Taeuber-Arp created a series of stylized marionettes that were small kinetic masterpieces. Now considered icons of Dada art, her puppets were a perfect example of her dancer's understanding of movement, her precise craftsmanship, and her playful approach to abstraction.

Taeuber-Arp worked at a time when applied art was looked down upon by the fine art world. This may help explain why she is not as famous as other artists in her circle—yet she was at the center of everything. Her astonishing creativity across disciplines is now being rediscovered and celebrated.

LYUBOV POPOVA

Trailblazing multimedia maven who merged art and politics

Lyubov Popova lived during a time of great artistic and political change. She was a creative force who worked in many different areas and always stretched herself—and art—in new directions. Though she died young, she left behind an enormous body of work that showed how art and politics can influence each other.

Popova was born into a wealthy family who supported her travels across Russia and around Europe to study art. She trained with cubist artists in France, then went to Italy and learned about futurism, a movement to sweep away artistic traditions and celebrate the new machine age. She returned to Russia and fused these styles together in colorful, abstract paintings full of movement and repetitive shapes.

She was part of a group of artists creating a distinctly Russian avant-garde style, blending the energy and geometry of modern art with elements of Russian folk art. After the Russian Revolution in 1917, Popova and her fellow artists thought that art should serve a social or practical purpose. Their ideas became known as constructivism, where artists became more like engineers who fused art and technology to look for solutions to modern social problems.

Leaving painting behind, Popova worked in textiles, graphic design, theater sets and costumes, books, and posters. She designed everyday objects meant for mass production. Her unique personal style wove basic geometric elements into complex patterns, bringing folk art into the future. A sense of motion was always her goal, from theater sets moving on giant cogs to fabrics with patterns that looked like optical illusions. She believed that art played an important part in moving society into a new future.

LYUBOV POPOVA

1889 – 1924

MOSCOW (RUSSIA)

EGON SCHIELE

1890 - 1918

TULLN (AUSTRIA)

ICONIC ARTISTS

EGON SCHIELE

Expressionist bad boy whose short career left a larger-than-life imprint on modern art

Egon Schiele left behind an astonishing amount of work when he died in the 1918 influenza pandemic at only 28 years old. On the surface, his skinny frame, messy hair, and disregard for society's rules marked him as an "art punk" poster boy. But the intense emotion of his exaggerated human forms—many of them self-portraits—had an enormous influence on modern art. More than 100 years after his death, Schiele is a mythical figure for fans of his dark, psychological work.

Schiele arrived in Vienna as a teenager to enroll in art school and found a mentor in Gustav Klimt, whose work he already admired. Klimt introduced him to the groundbreaking expressionist work of Vincent Van Gogh and Edvard Munch, as well as other current avant-garde movements. And though he was successful, Klimt stirred up controversy with the nudity in his work—just as Schiele would.

Frustrated with his conservative school, Schiele dropped out. He developed a sharp, angular style in his artwork, his bodies distorted but deeply expressive. He drew instinctively, at lightning speed. Once he was happy with a model's pose, it might take only two or three minutes to finish a sketch—often not even looking away from his model as he drew.

He had many admirers but stirred up trouble wherever he went. His bohemian lifestyle and the nudity in his art scandalized polite society and earned him run-ins with the law, including a judge who burned one of his paintings in court. While he was both celebrated and demonized in Vienna's art scene, he greatly influenced his contemporaries as well as later artists like Francis Bacon and Jean-Michel Basquiat. Many young artists today are as mesmerized by the raw power in Schiele's work as they are by his rule-breaking nature. Love him or hate him, he remains an icon.

ICONIC ARTISTS

ARCHIBALD MOTLEY

Artist who captured the color and rhythm of the Jazz Age and Black urban life

Archibald J. Motley, Jr. was one of the 20th century's most significant artists, though he is not as well-known as Edward Hopper or Georgia O'Keeffe. His striking and original visual language married classical techniques with the colorful and expressive values of modern art. By capturing the emotion and activity of everyday life in Black communities, he offered a perspective on American life that had long been ignored.

Motley was one of the first Black artists to enroll at the School of the Art Institute of Chicago, where he studied traditional European ideas and techniques. Racial tensions were high at the time, and Motley wanted to show that people's daily concerns were universal. With a bold, vivid style, he focused on scenes from Black urban life even as his portraits included people of different racial backgrounds and social classes. In 1929, he won a fellowship to study in Paris, and the color and rhythm of the city's cabarets electrified him. His work took on the moody blues and pinks of the cabaret lights, the vivid shades of Paris nightlife.

From a dynamic street scene in Chicago's Bronzeville neighborhood to a quiet portrait of his grandmother mending socks, Motley portrayed his subjects with a dignity and elegance missing from popular images of Black people in America. He purposefully challenged racial stereotypes, even when he used them himself.

Motley is often associated with the Harlem Renaissance, though he never lived in New York—Chicago was always his home and heart. His works echo with the energy and complexity of jazz music itself, a chronicle of 20th century American life.

ARCHIBALD MOTLEY

1891 – 1981

NEW ORLEANS, LOUISIANA (USA)

FORTUNATO DEPERO

The happy and energetic Italian futurist

Fortunato Depero wore many hats: he was a painter, a writer, a sculptor, and a graphic designer, to name just a few. Above all, he was true believer in futurism, a movement started in Italy in 1909 to celebrate the possibilities of the machine age and capture the spark of a new, fast-paced world of cars and airplanes. Depero developed a quirky, colorful style that resonated with movement, a wacky variation on cubism full of happy energy that reflected his sunny personality.

Depero knew he wanted to be an artist but was rejected from the fine arts academy he applied to. He moved to Rome and became part of the second wave of futurist artists. He wanted to make everything around him, from books to children's toys, into art objects. In 1919, he founded the House of Futurist Art, which designed and sold toys, furniture, and beautiful, intricate tapestries he called "cloth mosaics." He applied futurism's bold, sharp lines and sense of movement and progress to advertising, pushing graphic design forward with his crisp type and high contrast.

Depero arrived in New York in 1928, bringing with him a portfolio book called the *Depero Futurista* held together with two huge industrial bolts and considered the first modern-day artist's book. It contained page after page of Depero's favorite and most significant works, from his paintings and ads to pillows and toys, sprinkled with pages of futurist ideas about progress and technology. He attracted art directors and potential clients to his studio with his wife's homemade ravioli and other Italian dishes, then used his portfolio book to show them what he could do.

Italian futurism became tied to Fascist dictator Benito Mussolini and soon faded away, but its graphic visual language and push to bring fine art to everyday objects remained an influence in modern art. Depero was revolutionary for valuing all fields of art equally and working in them all: not only the "fine arts" of painting and sculpture, but architecture, theater, fashion, textiles, and more. This seems common for artists now, but in the 1920s, it made Depero a pioneer.

FORTUNATO DEPERO

1892 – 1960

TRENTINO (ITALY)

ICONIC ARTISTS

HENRY DARGER

Eccentric loner now celebrated as an epic self-taught genius

At age 80, a shy, eccentric man named Henry Darger moved to a nursing home from a room in Chicago he had rented for more than 40 years. When cleaning out the room, his landlord discovered one of the most astonishing collections of artwork in American art history. Darger had spent a lifetime building an imaginary world—thousands and thousands of pages of drawings, collages, and paintings.

More than 15,000 of those pages were hand-bound into seven large volumes, an epic story Darger called *The Story of the Vivian Girls, in What is Known as the Realms of the Unreal, of the Glandeco-Angelinian War Storm, Caused by the Child Slave Rebellion*. It is the surreal, *Odyssey*-like tale of the Vivian Girls as they fight to rescue innocent children from slavery and the evil of adults. Sprawling scenes in colored pencil and watercolor are crowded with characters against lush backgrounds, in pictures both fanciful and violent. Some of the book's pages were so long that they couldn't be unfolded flat in the apartment.

Darger's style is hard to define: part comic strip, part *Alice in Wonderland*, part dark Walt Disney and sprinkled with Catholic religious imagery. His images are both disturbing and beautiful, full of wonder, determination, and hope, along with darkness and pain. Without any art training at all, he used some of the same strategies found in works by surrealist or Dada artists.

Darger's art reflected many of the tragedies of his childhood. He was given up to an orphanage by his disabled father a few years after his mother died. He spent his teenage years in an abusive, crowded mental institution until he finally escaped for good. Described by others as pleasant but reclusive, it is thought that Darger never showed his art to anyone. Decades after his death, Henry Darger is now famous around the world as a genius of outsider, or self-taught, art.

HENRY DARGER

1892 – 1973

CHICAGO, ILLINOIS (USA)

PAULINE SIMON

1894 – 1976

MINSK (BELARUS)

PAULINE SIMON

Creator of enchanted feral pictures

As a girl in Russia (now Belarus), Pauline Simon would watch her mother trace floral patterns on frosted winter windows. Many decades later, this mostly self-taught painter produced visionary, romantic works full of patterns and textures, a fury of florals and folk art elements but with sly nods to some of modern art's great masters.

Simon lived an entire lifetime before taking up art. She immigrated to Chicago at the age of 18, working as a theatrical hairdresser until she married. She raised a family and managed her husband's dental office until his death in 1961. After her retirement at the age of 70, she took a painting class at the Art Institute of Chicago. Even without formal art training, Simon was no stranger to modern art. She and her husband had been lifetime members at the Art Institute, and she had spent decades studying the work of artists like Joan Miró and Gustav Klimt in its galleries.

Their vivid palettes and intense detailing influenced her own work. Every space on her canvases is filled with pattern and flowers and design elements, a joyful, romantic folk art style in rich, vibrant color. She combined the fluid, rhythmic forms of Henri Matisse with the painted-dot techniques of French pointillist Georges Seurat to create a fresh, individual approach.

Her wildly colorful, decorative style caught the attention of members of the Chicago Imagists. The Imagists were generally known for dense, figurative imagery, and though they were classically trained, they recognized many of the same qualities in Simon's paintings. They collected and promoted her work, and in 1974, Simon had her first solo art show at the Hyde Park Art Center, the community art center that had launched many of the Imagists' careers. She produced around 65 paintings between 1965 and her death in 1976. This wildly original late bloomer left behind a sparkling visual vocabulary all her own.

ICONIC ARTISTS

TAMARA DE LEMPICKA

The "baroness with a paintbrush" who captured the glamour of the Jazz Age

Tamara de Lempicka grew up in luxury: boarding school in Switzerland and summer trips to Italy. Newly married and living in St. Petersburg, the Russian Revolution ended her life of ease and landed her in Paris to start over. While she took up painting to feed her family, Lempicka became a symbol of the carefree spirit and glamour of the "roaring 20s." Her unique Art Deco style captured the decadence of the flapper era, but her greatest work of art might have been herself.

Lempicka combined sleek decoration with a "soft" version of cubism, still angular but less boxy. She painted liberated, lipsticked women and powerful, dapper men. Stylized versions of classical female nudes contrast against a sharp architectural background. Well-dressed and with every hair in place, she composed herself as carefully as her paintings. Her cool, chic paintings and glamorous personal style were perfect for Jazz Age Paris, and she quickly found success.

She befriended fashion designers and socialites, partying with and painting a who's-who of high society. Lempicka was one of the only portrait painters working in the new, trendy style of Art Deco, and her work was in high demand. When war loomed again in Europe, Lempicka convinced her new husband, a wealthy Hungarian baron, to move to California, where she was an immediate hit among the stars of Hollywood's silver screen.

Lempicka offered a new image of a modern woman, both on canvas and in person: strong and powerful but still sensual and feminine. Her distinctive style has influenced pop superstar Madonna and fashion designers like Karl Lagerfeld and Louis Vuitton. She painted the way she lived, on her own terms.

ICONIC ARTISTS

ALEXANDER CALDER

An artist as inventive as the circus that inspired him

Alexander Calder was born into art as the family business—both his parents and grandfather were successful artists. He grew up to be one of the most original and productive American artists of the 20th century, inventing the mobile and leaving his colorful, larger-than-life sculptures in cities around the world.

Calder studied engineering in college but quickly came back to art. Working as a magazine illustrator, he became fascinated with the shapes and motion of the circus after an assignment to draw the Ringling Bros. Circus. When he moved to Paris in 1926, he began making little circus figures from wire, fabric, and other found materials. He gave performances of his tiny Cirque Calder for friends, and soon people were paying to see his elaborate shows.

Calder was a born sculptor, "sketching" interesting people and scenes with wire rather than pencil and paper, creating drawings in the air. He had many friends among the Paris art set, and during a visit to Piet Mondrian's studio, Calder was struck by colorful cardboard rectangles tacked to the wall as experiments for future paintings. He suggested that it would be fun if the rectangles could rotate, but Mondrian wasn't interested. That visit changed his life. He was determined to bring movement to abstract art, and within a year, he invented his first kinetic sculpture—an entirely new type of art. He created floating shapes connected by wires that gently twisted and turned with the slightest air movement. It was fellow artist Marcel Duchamp who dubbed them "mobiles."

After years of going back and forth between Paris and New York, Calder moved back to the United States for good in 1933. He bought a Connecticut farmhouse with 18 acres of land and started experimenting with the large outdoor sculptures that became another of his hallmarks.

Calder made art all the time. He designed ballet sets and tapestries, painted murals, created jewelry, and made things for his family's home. He used red, yellow, blue, and black almost exclusively, combining bold colors and strong shapes to make art that still feels so fresh and original.

RENÉ MAGRITTE

1898 – 1967

LESSINES (BELGIUM)

ICONIC ARTISTS

RENÉ MAGRITTE

The undercover surrealist who turned everyday objects into mysteries

If Salvador Dalí was the wild man of surrealism, René Magritte was the quiet current running under its surface. In his bowler hat, grey suit, and dark coat, Magritte himself looked like an English banker. Yet he spent an entire career on the idea that appearances could be deceiving, turning everyday items into strange, mysterious symbols, and questioning the meaning of everything.

Magritte started painting as a teenager, but formal art classes bored him. A bigger influence was a classmate who introduced him to cubism and futurism. He worked as a commercial artist designing books, posters, and advertisements. He lived in Paris for a few years and connected with the surrealists, including Salvador Dalí and Max Ernst, but he wasn't drawn to the darker subjects many of them were exploring. Magritte returned to Brussels and to advertising but continued to paint, adding words and playing with language.

His style is clear and illustrative, full of familiar objects: clouds, apples, pipes. But Magritte placed them into unexpected scenes that made them look strange, even disturbing. He added words or contrasting objects that made his pictures into puzzles, such as his very famous *The Treachery of Images*, a painting of a pipe labeled with the French for "This is not a pipe." Magritte exposed the gap between language and meaning, representation and reality.

Magritte experimented with other styles over his career, but always came back to this realistic yet unsettling style. He believed that mystery lurks everywhere, even in the most unlikely places. His work influenced the pop artists of the 1960s and the conceptual artists of the 1980s, and continues to challenge us to see everything with fresh eyes.

LOUISE NEVELSON

1899 – 1988

KYIV (UKRAINE)

ICONIC ARTISTS

LOUISE NEVELSON

Visionary sculptor who broke through boundaries for women in abstract art

Determined and fiercely independent, Louise Nevelson was always ahead of her time. Her huge, abstract sculptures rocked the art world with their boldness. In later years she was a walking art presence in flowing caftans and dramatic false eyelashes, but she had the confidence of a legend long before the art world caught on.

As a young immigrant in Maine, Nevelson grew up dreaming of the New York art life. She married a wealthy businessman, but once in New York, he was not supportive of her art studies. Restless and unhappy, she left to study modern art in Germany but soon returned as political tensions rose in Europe.

She assisted with Diego Rivera's Rockefeller Center murals, then turned more to sculpture. She scavenged for scrap wood and other materials and pieced them together, influenced by cubist geometry and the "readymades" of Marcel Duchamp. Art buyers mostly ignored her—sculpture was for men.

On a trip to Mexico, Nevelson was stunned by the size and symbolism of Mayan monuments. Her work ballooned in size; she assembled entire walls of boxes full of nested objects. She painted them a single color, first black but later white, deep purple, or gold to explore shadow and space. Her constructions were dramatic and dreamlike, like a nighttime cityscape from above.

It was shocking for a woman to take up so much space, and her bravado finally brought attention to her work. She was a trailblazer of site-specific installations, sculptures designed for a certain space. She thought about how viewers would experience her work—an idea that spread in the 1960s and 70s but was rarely considered before.

Nevelson always had a sense of discovery, playing with unusual materials and experimenting with printmaking and collage. For Nevelson, making art was a conversation with her materials, improvising to find balance between her vision and what they wanted to become.

WILLIAM HENRY JOHNSON

1901 – 1970

FLORENCE, SOUTH CAROLINA (USA)

ICONIC ARTISTS

WILLIAM HENRY JOHNSON

Harlem Renaissance artist who created a powerful folk style to capture images of Black life

William Henry Johnson was the first Black American figurative painter to play with flat abstract shapes, creating a visual language that merged the simplicity of folk art with the complexity of jazz music. He depicted scenes of Black life during the Harlem Renaissance and the Great Migration, as millions of Black Americans left the rural South for cities in the North, Midwest, and West.

Johnson moved to New York from South Carolina at the age of 17. He worked a variety of jobs to attend the National Academy of Design, where he was such a talented student that teachers eventually raised money to send him to Europe. Studying the work of Vincent Van Gogh and the German expressionists spurred him to experiment with bolder colors and stronger lines. He became interested in folk art and culture while living in Scandinavia and traveling to North Africa with his new wife, a Danish textile and ceramics artist.

Johnson returned to New York as war became more likely in Europe. He taught art for the WPA, the New Deal program that employed millions of Americans during the Depression. He was part of a vibrant artistic community, learning screenprinting and refining a style of simplified forms and bright colors. Johnson focused his work on images of Black life, exploring the dual North/South perspective of the Great Migration and the forces that shaped it.

His career was cut short by the death of his wife in 1944. Grief sapped his mental and physical health, and Johnson spent the last 23 years of his life in a state hospital. His life's work was nearly destroyed after his death due to unpaid storage fees, but was fortunately rescued in time and donated to the Smithsonian American Art Museum.

WIFREDO LAM

1902 – 1982

SAGUA LA GRANDE (CUBA)

ICONIC ARTISTS

WIFREDO LAM

Cuban artist who challenged Western assumptions about non-European art

Wifredo Lam, born to a Chinese father and an Afro-Cuban mother of Spanish descent, was a pivotal figure in Latin American modern art. By drawing on influences from both sides of the Atlantic Ocean, he created a cross-cultural visual language that was all his own.

After studying painting and sculpture as a young man, Lam won a scholarship to study in Madrid and stayed there for many years before moving to Paris. He was welcomed into the Parisian art scene, becoming friends with Pablo Picasso and spending time with other leading artists like André Breton and Joan Miró. He visited Diego Rivera and Frida Kahlo in Mexico. He experimented with cubist techniques and surrealist ideas, influenced by the African art popular in Paris at the time, including Picasso's own collection of masks.

When the Germans invaded Paris during World War II, Lam returned to Cuba and reconnected with his homeland. After many years away, he was deeply upset by the corruption and racial inequality he saw. He began exploring themes of social injustice and spirituality with large-scale paintings combining modernist techniques with images of mask-like faces and jungle vegetation in the earthy and vibrant colors of the Caribbean. He once said, "I wanted with all my heart to paint the drama of my country," and he mined the whole rich and complex cultural history of Cuba for inspiration.

Lam thought of himself as a kind of artistic Trojan horse, using the language of European modernism to bring attention to Cuba's African heritage and the effects of colonialism. His unique multicultural style demonstrated deep respect for the African traditions that inspired him, paving the way for later Black artists to reclaim their heritage in their work. Lam was a true innovator who challenged assumptions and resisted labels.

JOSEPH CORNELL

1903 – 1972

NYACK, NEW YORK (USA)

JOSEPH CORNELL

Self-taught artist whose shadow boxes contained worlds of imagination

A shy, bookish man, Joseph Cornell rarely left the small home in New York City that he shared with his aging mother and disabled younger brother. His imagination, however, was too big to contain, and the art boxes he created were miniature universes of controlled wonder.

Cornell had no art training, but he was interested in arts and culture of all types and spent his time in bookshops, movie houses, museums, and galleries. He brought home tiny treasures from his excursions, collecting and cataloging everything from old pictures and maps to watch springs, shells, and corks. In 1931, he saw collages by the surrealist Max Ernst and realized that art could be more than paint on canvas. He experimented with his own collages, cutting illustrations out of old books. His work was so original and striking that the following year, he was included in the first surrealist gallery exhibition in the US.

He soon started to combine collage with objects from his ever-growing collection, often manipulating them to look like Victorian-era antiques and placing them in shallow glass-fronted boxes. Cornell said his shadow boxes were based on "the beauty of the commonplace," but the way he combined seemingly unrelated images often gave them a magical, dreamlike quality. He explored themes of childhood, curiosity, music, and travel with images that mingle fantasy and reality in unexpected ways.

Cornell's ethereal, fantastic shadow boxes drew the world to his door. He became good friends with Ernst, Marcel Duchamp, and Mark Rothko. Younger artists including Andy Warhol, Robert Rauschenberg, and Yayoi Kusuma were regular visitors. Russian ballerina Tamara Toumanova sent him bits of her costumes in exchange for his gifts of artwork. A "master of ceremonies" of the imagination, Cornell made art that continues to enchant viewers and defy categorization.

SALVADOR DALÍ

1904 – 1989

FIGUERES (SPAIN)

SALVADOR DALÍ

Clown prince of surrealism and master of self-promotion

Salvador Dalí is surely one of the most famous artists of the 20th century, with his cartoonish waxed mustache and wide-eyed stare. He was a prankster and agitator who was also a masterful painter of haunting dreamlike images. His carefully invented persona erased the line between art and artist long before artists were expected to become "brands."

Dalí's talent appeared at a young age, but he had a terrible temper and was expelled from art school for insulting his professors. A trip to Paris changed his life. He met Pablo Picasso and was inspired by the cubist and futurist movements, along with Sigmund Freud's ideas about the subconscious mind.

Fellow Spaniard Joan Miró introduced him to the surrealists of Paris, who believed that intuition, not conscious thought, should guide their work. Dalí went further, creating a disoriented state of mind on purpose to connect unrelated things in what he called "hand-painted dream photographs." He painted hyper-realistic staircases, keys, dripping candles, and of course, melting clocks—symbols for big ideas like death, hope, and time.

Dalí was a natural showman and loved controversy, which helped his commercial success but hurt his reputation in the art world. He created jewelry and furniture, designed store windows and theater sets, and wrote fiction and essays. He collaborated with filmmakers Walt Disney and Alfred Hitchcock.

Critics and art fans still argue about whether Dalí was a genius or a madman. He said shocking things in support of European dictators but claimed he was not interested in politics. He was a visual joker who crowned his seaside home (and later his museum) with massive egg sculptures. But he also broke new ground for artists to add more mystery and emotion into their work. His work still captures the imagination.

LOÏS MAILOU JONES

1905 – 1998

BOSTON, MASSACHUSETTS (USA)

ICONIC ARTISTS

LOÏS MAILOU JONES

Versatile painter, designer, and mentor who broke new ground for Black artists

Loïs Mailou Jones started her art career as a fabric designer. She created beautiful textiles for companies in Boston and New York, playful abstract nature patterns and colorful designs inspired by African and Caribbean motifs. She liked seeing her designs in shop windows, but only a pattern's name was printed on the fabric—not the artist who created it.

Jones wanted more recognition for all her hard work, so she turned her focus to painting. She became an art professor at Howard University and spent summers immersed in the art of the Harlem Renaissance depicting Black lives and experiences. She was one of the first Black artists to use African masks and designs in her paintings, as a tribute and link between the past and the future for people of African heritage.

After teaching for several years, Jones spent a year studying in Paris, where she was energized by the acceptance of French society compared to the racism she endured in the US. Many American galleries and painting competitions did not accept Black artists. When she returned home, a white friend would pretend to be Jones to deliver paintings and accept awards that Jones won for her work.

In the 1950s, she started traveling to her husband's home country of Haiti and took inspiration from the vibrant colors and patterns there. She also traveled regularly to Africa, visiting studios and conducting interviews, not only to develop her own work but to take pictures and document the work of African artists.

Jones painted an incredible variety of subjects and styles, from New England landscapes to African tribal patterns, always with a strong sense of color and design. She was a dedicated mentor to her students and worked hard to create opportunities for other Black artists. Her work now hangs in museums around the world as a testament to her determination and talent.

LEE GODIE

Chicago's grand queen of self-taught art

In 1968, a woman appeared on the steps of the Art Institute of Chicago in a patchwork fur coat, selling paintings for just a few dollars to museum visitors and art school students. She called herself a French impressionist and claimed to be "much better than Cézanne." For the next 20 years, Lee Godie was a force of nature, blurring the lines between art and life even as she worked and often lived on the streets.

Self-taught, Godie said that it was a little red bird who first told her to pick up a brush. After that, her life centered around art and the concept of beauty, a stark contrast to her harsh life. She painted bold, intense portraits of stylish women and handsome men. She often painted birds with phrases like "Hurry Spring" or "Chicago, We Own It." She took hundreds of self-portraits in a bus station photo booth, using props like a bouquet of roses or a silver goblet to transform herself into the beauties she painted. She would attach these photos to her paintings as a visual signature.

Buying a painting directly from Godie became part of the experience, as she was particular about who deserved to buy her work. With charm, toughness, and a larger-than-life personality, she became Chicago's most collected artist, a living legend, and had many loyal friends who looked out for her as she chose to continue living in parks and on the streets.

Godie was very private about her life before becoming an artist, but it is known that she suffered several personal tragedies. Toward the end of her life, her daughter found her, and they formed a new relationship. Godie's life ended comfortably, reconnected with family. After her passing, her work made the journey to France, the adopted country of her heart, as part of a large exhibition of outsider art from Chicago collections.

LEE GODIE

1908 – 1994

CHICAGO, ILLINOIS (USA)

LEE KRASNER & JACKSON POLLOCK

Abstract expressionism's dynamic couple who paved a new path in art

In 1949, *Life* magazine ran a story asking, "Jackson Pollock: Is he the greatest living painter in the United States?" He had one of the most radically abstract styles in modern art's history, his drip paintings full of emotion without any recognizable subject. But while Pollock worked in his barn studio, his wife, Lee Krasner, painted her own masterpieces in a spare bedroom.

Lee Krasner grew up in New York constantly fighting for opportunities to study and exhibit in a very male-dominated art world. She was drawn to avant-garde styles and began to cover entire canvases with repetitive, "all-over" abstract patterns. Pollock had followed two older brothers to New York in 1930. He studied Old Masters and mural painting before creating more abstract drawings influenced by Pablo Picasso, Joan Miró, and surrealist ideas about the subconscious.

Krasner and Pollock became a couple following a gallery show that included them both. All eyes in the art world were on New York, where abstract expressionists like Krasner and Pollock were creating the first truly American modern art movement. Krasner devoted herself to Pollock's career, marketing him to galleries and art collectors like a manager would today. She let her own career fade into the background as his star rose, but she never stopped making art.

While their relationship could be difficult at times, mostly due to Pollock's alcoholism, Pollock believed in Krasner's talent as much as she did in his. Where many expressionists stuck to a signature style, Krasner cycled through new ones, too full of ideas to stay in one place visually. Some of her best pieces were mosaics made from cut-up pieces of old paintings she wasn't satisfied with.

Pollock died in 1956, but Krasner continued to make art for more than 20 years. The women's movement of the 1960s and '70s brought her work more into the spotlight, and her contributions to modern art became better known. Together, this dynamic couple broke new ground with some of the most original work of the 20th century.

JACKSON POLLOCK

1912 – 1956

CODY, WYOMING (USA)

LEE KRASNER

1908 – 1984

NEW YORK, NEW YORK (USA)

REMEDIOS VARO

1908 – 1963

ANGLÉS (SPAIN)

ICONIC ARTISTS

REMEDIOS VARO

Spanish-Mexican painter of haunting magical mysteries

Spanish-born artist Remedios Varo blurred the lines between fantasy and reality with a blend of traditional techniques, surrealist philosophy, and an interest in the supernatural. Her haunting, highly individual work weaves stories full of medieval references and scientific symbols, with wide-eyed main characters that often look like Varo herself.

Varo grew up in a household swirling with science and religion. Her engineer father gave her books on philosophy and science, while her mother was a devoted Catholic who sent her to convent school. She studied painting at a very traditional school (Salvador Dalí was expelled the year she arrived) but was drawn to the surrealist interest in the unconscious mind and the disturbing, dreamlike paintings of Hieronymus Bosch. She made friends with the surrealist artists of Paris and Barcelona but found little success in the very male European art world.

When she settled in Mexico in 1941, she finally found an artistic community where her talent could shine. Varo, photographer Kati Horna, and fellow painter Leonora Carrington became known as the "three witches" for their intense interest in Indigenous spirituality and supernatural rituals. She painted dreamscapes of science fiction imagery set in a mystical enchanted forest. Her figures, often a single woman in long robes, are at work on a project, a game, or a scientific discovery. Medieval references are common, like the one-room buildings on wheels used for traveling miracle plays or the glass globes of alchemy.

Varo explored the magical and mystical, the unseen world, and the occult sense of metamorphosis. When she died at the height of her career in 1963, André Breton, one of the founders of surrealism, called her "the sorceress who left too soon." She is now considered one of the most extraordinary painters of Mexican surrealism.

ICONIC ARTISTS

GERTRUDE ABERCROMBIE

The queen of Chicago surrealism

Gertrude Abercrombie, born to a pair of traveling opera singers, was still a young girl when her family settled in Chicago's Hyde Park neighborhood. Her roots remained there for the rest of her life, and while Abercrombie was well-known at home in the 1940s and '50s, it is only recently that her art has become more widely appreciated. Her unique style borrows from surrealism and magical realism to explore dreams, the supernatural, and the very nature of the world.

Abercrombie studied briefly at the Art Institute of Chicago and the American Academy of Art, but was mostly self-taught. She started her art career illustrating gloves for department store advertisements. In her mid-20s, she began painting more seriously, peculiar small self-portraits and pictures of ladders, moons, owls, shells, and other objects. She painted eerie, flat landscapes layered with mysterious symbols, nothing like the abstract modernism or Midwestern realism trendy in art circles. She had a visual language all her own.

Abercrombie became known as "the queen of the bohemian artists," gathering all sorts of Chicago creatives and visiting artists. She entertained jazz musicians like Charlie Parker and Sarah Vaughan and would often improvise with them on the piano. Her Hyde Park home was known as a safe haven for traveling jazz artists at a time when many Black musicians were turned away by hotels.

"Queen Gertrude," as her close friends called her, was an eccentric character, driving a used Rolls Royce and often wearing a pointy black hat and a cape. Her paintings are also wonderfully odd, suggesting fantastical stories of mystery. She often drew inspiration from her own dreams, and like a dream, her images are vivid and clear but in a way that feels just out of reach. The great Dizzy Gillespie, one of Abercrombie's closest friends, compared her paintings to jazz music itself.

GERTRUDE ABERCROMBIE

1909 – 1977

AUSTIN, TEXAS (USA)

ICONIC ARTISTS

CORITA KENT

The pop art nun who tried to make the world better with her art

Pop art is known for bright, bold color, but one of its greatest artists was a Catholic nun in a black-and-white habit. Corita Kent's messages of love, peace, and kindness rocked the world of poster art then, and still resonate today.

Sister Mary Corita taught drawing and painting at Immaculate Heart College, a progressive school in Los Angeles. She brought in avant-garde artists like John Cage and Charles Eames, and the school was abuzz with creative thinking. As a practicing artist, she was getting attention for her screenprinting, mostly religious subjects with many more layers of color than usual.

Seeing Andy Warhol's *Soup Can* paintings in 1962 changed everything for her. She was electrified by the clean lines and bold colors of pop art. She started using ad slogans, song lyrics, and other bits of pop culture to get social justice ideas out to a large audience. She printed on common materials and sold her work by mail to make it accessible.

Her exuberant work shook up the church and the art world—she was even on the cover of *Newsweek*. But though Kent's work was rooted in her faith, she faced intense criticism from conservative voices in the Catholic Church that thought her art was "weird and sinister." Eventually worn out by the church's disapproval and her busy schedule, she left the order in 1968 but continued making prints about poverty, civil rights, and the anti-war movement.

Not since Toulouse-Lautrec had anyone used poster art as such a complete record of the era they lived in. Kent's themes of peace and social justice, expressed in bright, bold Day-Glo colors, still feel very relevant today.

CORITA KENT

1918 – 1986

FORT DODGE, IOWA (USA)

ICONIC ARTISTS

RUTH ASAWA

Artist, activist, and educator who brought new organic forms to sculpture

Ruth Asawa's mother, a Japanese immigrant and farmer, drilled the values of *gaman* (endurance), *nintai* (patience), and *enryo* (restraint) into her children. Asawa's modernist wire sculptures reflect a lifetime of putting those values into practice, even in the face of adversity and injustice.

Asawa worked long and hard as a small child, with farm duties before and after school. Even then, her young artist's eyes found inspiration that stayed with her: "I used to sit on the back of the horse-drawn leveler with my bare feet drawing forms in the sand, which later in life became the bulk of my sculptures." As a teenager, Asawa and her family were forced into US internment camps for people of Japanese ancestry. She continued to study drawing with several Disney animators also imprisoned there.

On her release, Asawa studied to be an art teacher but was denied a certificate because she was Japanese-American. Disappointed, she went with friends to Black Mountain College in North Carolina. The creative atmosphere there was electric. She studied with Bauhaus painter Josef Albers and architect R. Buckminster Fuller.

On a trip to Mexico, Asawa learned wire weaving and began to create looped-wire sculptures inspired by coral, insects, and other forms in nature. Her delicate, airy forms, usually hung from the ceiling, were a new type of sculpture, intricate works that could be very large without heaviness.

In addition to her art career, Asawa was an activist for arts education in the public schools of San Francisco, her adopted hometown. Faced with racial discrimination and sexist attitudes, Asawa's work was ignored by art historians for many years, but she is now celebrated as an innovator and educator.

RUTH ASAWA

1926 – 2013

NORWALK, CALIFORNIA (USA)

ANDY WARHOL

The king of pop art who made celebrity itself into fine art

As a kid with health issues, Andy Warhol spent a lot of his time in bed reading movie magazines and drawing. This shy, dreamy boy grew up to define celebrity culture, reinventing himself into a cultural phenomenon and one of America's most famous artists.

American art in the 1940s and '50s was very abstract, and some artists wanted to bring recognizable images back into art. Warhol had a very successful career as a commercial illustrator, and a gallery owner suggested that he paint everyday items. His now-iconic series of 32 Campbell's soup cans used fine art techniques to paint a mass-produced object, introducing one of the main ideas of the new pop art movement.

Pop art used images from the media and popular culture to break down lines between high and low art—and to question what counted as art at all. Along with other pop artists like Roy Lichtenstein and Robert Rauschenberg, Warhol played with scale and held up an artistic mirror to the culture and consumerism of the 1960s.

Warhol thought that the way Hollywood "manufactured" celebrities was not so different from items on a grocery store shelf. He used silkscreening to create multiple images of stars like Marilyn Monroe, bringing the idea of mass production to the art piece itself. He carried this idea further, naming his studio The Factory and using assistants to produce work under his direction. He expanded into movies, making more than 650 films that laid the groundwork for the independent film industry.

This introverted gay kid from an immigrant Pittsburgh neighborhood was perhaps his own greatest creation. He turned a persona into an international brand, carving out a new kind of fame and celebrity for an artist.

ANDY WARHOL

1928 – 1987

PITTSBURGH, PENNSYLVANIA (USA)

MARISOL ESCOBAR

1930 – 2016

PARIS (FRANCE)

ICONIC ARTISTS

MARISOL ESCOBAR

Elegant and enigmatic sculptor who fused folk art and pop art

Sculptor Marisol Escobar was born María Sol Escobar to a wealthy Venezuelan family that traveled often between Europe, Venezuela, and the US. She moved to New York in 1950 and studied drawing and painting before focusing on sculpture. She quickly became one of the most popular artists of her time, her sharply funny block figures drawing huge gallery crowds and her glamorous look landing her on the cover of fashion magazines.

    Escobar's first sculptures were small pieces in clay, bronze, or wood, but as her work got attention, it also got bigger. She started to carve life-size wooden figures and embellish them with fabric, paint, and found objects. She brought together ancient Central and South American folk art and the collages of modern artists like Robert Rauschenberg into elegant, block-like forms seemingly frozen in time.

    Escobar was part of the pop art scene of 1960s New York, appearing in several Andy Warhol movies and exhibiting along other pop artists, but her work never quite fit in. She had some elements in common with pop art, like her use of celebrity images, but her pieces were also very personal, based on her own emotions and experiences. Many were satirical, poking fun at women's social roles. She often used plaster casts of her own hands and face to finish her figures.

    People were as fascinated with Escobar's mysterious persona as they were with her art. As a child, she had mostly stopped talking for years after her mother died and preferred to communicate with her art more than with words. She would disappear from the art world for long periods of traveling but continued to make art even when her celebrity faded. Her genre-bending style and "forget the rules" attitude appeals to a generation now rediscovering her work.

ICONIC ARTISTS

BAYA MAHIEDDINE

North African teenager whose lush, vivid style influenced some of the biggest names in Paris

The art of Baya Mahieddine, who preferred just "Baya" for her art, has been described many ways over the years: surrealist, outsider, naïve. But this self-taught Algerian artist rejected European art-world categories. She painted from her own experience and stayed true to her unique vision, calling her style simply, "Baya-ism."

Born Fatma Haddad, Baya had lost her parents and was living with her grandmother when her artistic talent was noticed by a French art collector living in Algiers. The woman became Baya's guardian and showed her work to connections in the Paris art scene. Baya had her first solo exhibition in Paris weeks before she turned 16, and her work was a sensation among some of Paris's biggest names, including Henri Matisse, Jean Dubuffet, and surrealism founder André Breton.

Baya drew on the rich patterns of Algerian textiles, pottery, and architecture with a bold, "more-is-more" style. The women in her paintings—Baya never painted men—are expressive and confident, often looking directly back at the viewer. Most male artists painted women only as objects of beauty, so the emotion and spirit of Baya's subjects was unusual. They inhabit lively, colorful dreamscapes full of birds, fruit, instruments, and flowers, with a sense of energy and freedom.

Her strong, fluid style influenced the older, more famous artists around her. Her bright colors crept into their palettes. She spent several summers working with Pablo Picasso at a ceramics studio in the south of France, where he was spurred on by her endless creativity. Baya stopped painting for about 10 years when she was a young mother and Algeria was at war, but returned to painting in the mid-1960s. She remained an independent spirit, always true to her roots and to herself.

BAYA MAHIEDDINE

1931 – 1998

BORDJ EL KIFFAN (ALGERIA)

ICONIC ARTISTS

NAM JUNE PAIK

The "Father of Video Art" and prophet of the digital age who bridged the gap between art and technology

In 1954, Nam June Paik's family bought the first TV in their entire neighborhood. Paik's fascination with technology never left him, and the way his work captured both the potential and the dangers of the coming digital age made him into one of the first truly global artists. Through sculpture, performance, music, and installations, Paik became the founding father of video art.

Trained as a classical pianist, Paik studied music and art history before going to West Germany, the center of avant-garde music and performance. He was deeply influenced by the work of artists he befriended there, like composer John Cage's use of everyday sounds and Joseph Beuys's interactive performance art. Paik was surrounded by artists blending different media and erasing lines dividing art and everyday life.

Paik began playing with video when the first portable videotape recorder became available. He moved to New York in 1964 and started creating performances mixing music and video, often working with other artists. He worked with an engineer to invent one of the first machines that enabled an artist to change and manipulate existing video. He built massive sculptures from stacks of broken or heavily modified television monitors.

Paik was born in Korea and as a teenager moved with his family to Hong Kong and then Japan to escape the Korean War. His travels around the world made him question how technology crossed borders and cultures. He invented the phrase "electronic superhighway" to explain how communication, not transportation, would connect the modern world.

With humor and playfulness, Paik's work always tried to humanize technology, from an early robot sculpture that "pooped" dried beans to televisions worn like a bra. He wanted us to understand technology in order to keep it from controlling us: "I use technology," he said, "in order to hate it properly."

NAM JUNE PAIK

1932 – 2006

SEOUL (SOUTH KOREA)

ICONIC ARTISTS

ED PASCHKE

Mr. Chicago's intense, surreal paintings took pop art to new and darker places

If Alexander Calder "ran away to the circus" by making his toy sculptures, one could argue that Ed Paschke never made it past the sideshow. Paschke painted dark yet often endearing curiosities: smiling tattooed ladies, barrel-chested wrestlers, an accordion-playing family with glow-in-the-dark faces. His subjects could be intentionally weird or creepy, but Paschke portrayed them with affection and a sense of humor.

Paschke was part of a loose movement in the late 1960s called the Chicago Imagists, graduates of the School of the Art Institute of Chicago. The Chicago Imagists were inspired by underground comic books, surrealism, pop culture, and Andy Warhol. Paschke was especially interested in the margins of society and the darker side of urban life, filming or taking pictures of people he found interesting or strange for inspiration.

Paschke's portraits have exaggerated, sometimes zombie-like features. Famous historical figures or celebrities are distorted with clashing neon colors and the static patterns of late-night TV. Paschke was interested in the ways that mass media shapes reality, and often projected snippets from TV or magazines onto his work that he would then paint over—one of the first artists to use this technique.

Over his many decades as a working artist, he constantly experimented with new ways to make his arresting images, adding simple video, holograms, and photography. He was well-known and well-loved in his hometown of Chicago, a professor who was generous with his time and a kind, thoughtful advocate for art. But he was first and foremost an innovator, one of the first to translate the visual language of the digital world into oil paint on canvas.

ED PASCHKE

1939 – 2004

CHICAGO, ILLINOIS (USA)

ORLAN

*Radical multimedia artist whose
raw material is her own body*

French multimedia artist ORLAN is a living work of art, using her own body as her canvas. Pushing at the edges of how art is defined, she uses every moment to question ideas about beauty, identity, and modern society. Often controversial, ORLAN's art is designed to be shocking, even disturbing, making us question how we see the human body and the possibilities of technology.

ORLAN uses fine art methods including photography, video, and sculpture, but also tools from science and technology like robotics and artificial reality. In the early 1990s, she started a series of performances during which she had her appearance surgically altered, sometimes to reference famous paintings but always to make herself less like the "ideal" standard of beauty. She has always been particularly interested in how women's bodies have been controlled and judged throughout history.

More recently, she created a robot modeled on herself that could dance and speak with her voice, an entirely new idea of the artist's self-portrait. She invited developers to create new hardware and software to add to the robot, further blurring the line between her real identity and a virtual version.

ORLAN shares few details about her past and her personal life, presenting her work as her entire public identity. She is a complete self-invention, with no boundary between life and art—a prankster, a thinker, and an innovator. Like iconic artists before her, she upsets established ideas to challenge how we see the world around us.

ORLAN

Born 1947

SAINT-ÉTIENNE (FRANCE)

MR. IMAGINATION

1948 – 2012

MAYWOOD, ILLINOIS (USA)

ICONIC ARTISTS

MR. IMAGINATION

Visionary folk artist who transformed bottlecaps into jewels

One of nine children in a tough Chicago neighborhood, Gregory Warmack grew up as resourceful as he was artistic, painting rocks and carving little masks from tree bark. He spent his teens and 20s making and selling jewelry, hats, and other items on the street and at local venues. Everything changed when he was shot and nearly killed in a robbery at age 30, spending six weeks in a coma. He saw visions and felt a spiritual calling to make art with a positive impact on the world. After his recovery, he adopted the name Mr. Imagination and approached his art with new purpose and determination.

Mr. Imagination saw joy and possibility in found objects, transforming old brooms and discarded paint brushes into mask-like sculptures. He carved Egyptian kings from castoff sandstone. He constructed totem poles and chairs like thrones, then bejeweled them with rhinestones and his most-used material, recycled bottlecaps. He worked in an intuitive, organic way, bringing new life and meaning to common and overlooked materials with his detailed and colorful work.

He created large, wondrous folk-art environments for music venues, universities, and other public areas, leaving a "trail of decoration" wherever he went. He believed so strongly in the transformative power of art that when he lost his home and much of his work to a fire in 2009, he used burnt pieces to make new ones.

To Mr. Imagination, art was a force for empowerment and social change. He gave art workshops for children and senior citizens and mentored young artists from many different backgrounds. He was a nonstop creative force, and his work in galleries and museums across the country proves his reputation as one of America's most creative, visionary artists.

DAVID McDERMOTT

Born 1952

HOLLYWOOD, CALIFORNIA (USA)

PETER McGOUGH

Born 1958

SYRACUSE, NEW YORK (USA)

ICONIC ARTISTS

DAVID McDERMOTT & PETER McGOUGH

The Edwardian gentlemen of 1980s New York

David McDermott and Peter McGough went to the same university but didn't cross paths until they were both living in New York in 1980. McDermott & McGough, as they became known, were the time travelers of the East Village art world, as famous for their historical lifestyle as for their paintings, film, sculpture, and photography.

When they met, McDermott was already well-known in the downtown club scene for his antique manners and odd vintage clothes like a top hat and tails. Together, they were soon creating a sort of Edwardian bubble, living as gentlemen from the early 1900s in an apartment with no modern conveniences like electricity or appliances. They made their entire lives into a work of art in what they called "time experiments."

McDermott & McGough used old-fashioned techniques and materials like cyanotype, salt, platinum, and palladium in their photographs and paintings. Their work borrowed imagery and objects from the turn of the century, and they even backdated their paintings. But their themes were of-the-moment: popular culture, consumerism, gay identity, and the AIDS crisis. They questioned the nature of time and American disposable culture.

McDermott & McGough filled their home with period antiques and wallpaper—then documented it. They owned a horse and carriage and drove a 1913 Model T car. They drew people into their world, partying with fashion designers, models, and musicians. McDermott & McGough were the darlings of the 1980s art world, rubbing shoulders with Julian Schnabel, Keith Haring, and Jean-Michel Basquiat.

Eventually, the IRS came knocking—they had never paid taxes on all that success. They moved to Ireland, though McGough returned to New York a few years later. They continued to collaborate across the Atlantic for more than 20 years before parting creative ways. McGough continues to paint and make art, no longer limited to a single historical time period.

KEITH HARING

1958 – 1990

READING, PENNSYLVANIA (USA)

KEITH HARING

Street artist and activist whose quirky cartoon style defined the 1980s

Keith Haring loved drawing cartoons as a kid. He held onto that sense of fun and energy as he became an adult, and his style is now recognized around the world. He was a powerful visual communicator who used his art to spread joy and work for social change.

Haring came to New York to study at the School of Visual Arts, but he quickly discovered the alternative street art scene, becoming friends with graffiti artist Jean-Michel Basquiat. He used blank advertising spaces in the subway as his canvas, drawing flying saucers, crawling babies, barking dogs, and giant hearts in bold white chalk lines. He made thousands of these public drawings and started to get noticed, a club kid from the downtown art scene eventually moving into art exhibits and gallery shows.

A solo exhibition in 1982 propelled his work into worldwide recognition. He traveled the world creating murals and public art, and seeing the art of ancient cultures like the Mayans and Aborigines up close influenced his work. He worked with 900 children on a mural for the Statue of Liberty's 100th birthday and painted a chunk of the Berlin Wall.

Haring was an activist as well as an artist. He tackled heavy subjects like the AIDS epidemic and South African apartheid, but used bold, vivid colors and his bouncy cartoonish style to get his message across to a wide audience. Catchy slogans like "Crack is Wack" and "Silence = Death" left no doubt that his lively paintings meant serious business.

Haring believed strongly that art is for everybody. In 1986, he opened the Pop Shop to make his work more accessible by putting it on posters, T-shirts, and other small collectibles. His art was everywhere; he worked with pop stars like Madonna, fashion designers like Vivienne Westwood, and consumer brands like Swatch and Absolut. Like his friend Andy Warhol, he blended pop culture and fine art into a style that defined a decade.

NICK CAVE

Born 1959

FULTON, MISSOURI (USA)

ICONIC ARTISTS

NICK CAVE

Creator of art that moves, dances, jumps, delights, and challenges everything

Nick Cave calls himself a messenger, artist, and educator, in that order, and twines these roles together in everything he does. His work is impossible to put into a category, crossing sculpture, fashion, performance, dance, video, and more. Cave is a visual pioneer, but he is also carving out new ways of practicing art.

The third of seven boys, Cave learned early on how to repurpose his brothers' hand-me-downs and work with whatever materials were around. His family was not well off, but they were resourceful and creative, bringing imagination and togetherness into everyday life. Cave now brings those qualities to his art.

Cave is best known for his Soundsuits, elaborate full-body costumes that often make noise as they move. His first was created in response to the 1991 police beating of Rodney King; he collected discarded twigs and sticks and assembled them into a kind of protective armor. Soundsuits cover the wearer completely so that viewers can look without making judgements about race, class, or gender. A cacophony of crazy colors and found materials—from beads and hair to sock monkeys—Soundsuits are wearable sculptures that can be beautiful, even playful, but address serious issues of identity, racism, and violence.

Cave has a gift for dazzling the eye while asking difficult questions. His multimedia sculptures, performances, and public installations take a hard look at bigotry while exploring the ways art can bring people together for a more joyful future. He has involved community and social service groups in his performances for many years and is passionate about mentoring his students and creating opportunities for younger artists. With his partner and frequent collaborator Bob Faust, Cave recently opened Facility, a studio, gallery, and performance space. Cave continues to find new ways to ask, "How do you want to exist in the world, and how are you going to do the work?"

JEAN-MICHEL BASQUIAT

1960 – 1988

BROOKLYN, NEW YORK (USA)

JEAN-MICHEL BASQUIAT

Artist who rocked the art world with his confrontational style mixing street art with fine art

Jean-Michel Basquiat was a 1980s New York Renaissance man—a musician, a poet, a graffiti artist, a club DJ—but it's his paintings that brought him fame. Decades after his death, he is a pop icon, name-checked by hip-hop artists and collected by Hollywood stars. His fierce visual-collage style and biting social commentary shook up the art world then and are still relevant and influential today.

Born to parents of Puerto Rican and Haitian heritage, Basquiat spoke three languages and was a bright and curious child who loved roaming New York's many art museums with his mother. But life at home was not easy, and Basquiat left at 17 to stay with friends or on the street, sometimes selling hand-painted postcards and t-shirts.

Basquiat first got attention for his graffiti art, social and political messages tagged with the name SAMO. He brought the same raw, edgy style to canvas, mixing different styles and often adding words. He used recurring symbols like skulls, feet, bats, and a three-pointed crown in a kind of modern hieroglyphics. Some critics thought his sketch-like style looked simple, but Basquiat layered in references to art history, jazz music, and Black cultural heroes in an expressive new way.

Basquiat bridged many different worlds. He was a star of the downtown art scene, friends with Keith Haring and collaborating with Andy Warhol. But he was critical of the art world's lack of people of color, so he also spent time with graffiti and hip-hop artists in the Bronx and Harlem. His paintings often explored racism, classism, and other areas of tension or opposition.

His work was fearless and confrontational even as he became a star. Basquiat struggled with addiction and died of a drug overdose at age 27. In the years since, his short but iconic career continues to inspire musicians and fashion designers as well as modern artists like Shepard Fairey and Banksy.

ICONIC ARTISTS

MICKALENE THOMAS

Multidisciplinary artist putting Black women in the spotlight

When Mickalene Thomas was in art school, she couldn't always afford expensive oil paint, so she shopped at the craft supplies store. She used felt, rhinestones, yarn, and glitter to create beautiful and powerful portraits of her friends and family, as well as subjects from vintage photographs. She is now one of the art stars of her generation, a multi-talented, multi-disciplinary artist whose work crosses painting, film, collage, photography, fashion, and theater.

Thomas didn't always want to be an artist. She was studying pre-law and theater when she went to see a photography exhibit by Carrie Mae Weems called the *Kitchen Table* Series. Weems's work put a Black woman front and center in a way she had never seen before, and she knew she had found her calling. Thomas moved to New York to study art soon after.

Fine art has historically used Black women as symbols or objects—when showing them at all. Thomas presents women of color as main characters comfortable in their own spaces, with all their humanity, complexity, and dignity intact. She highlights their beauty, glamour, and power, drawing on influences ranging from Pablo Picasso and Édouard Manet to 1970s movies and fashion. Her work moves past representation into celebration, treating her subjects with gratitude and asking questions about who has been left out of the stories history tells.

Thomas sees art as an act of love and community and puts that idea into practice. She makes a point of supporting other artists, including mentoring younger ones—connecting the past with the present and future, just as she does in her work. Thomas makes work that, without apology, demands that Black women be seen and understood. She is helping to push the art world—and society—toward a more inclusive future.

MICKALENE THOMAS

Born 1971

CAMDEN, NEW JERSEY (USA)

BISA BUTLER

Portrait artist turning the often-overlooked quilt into the finest art

Bisa Butler's portraits are riots of color, vividly detailed and larger than life, yet created without a brush or paint. With fabric and thread, she "paints" richly textured stories of African ancestry, American history, and individual identity in bright Kool-Aid colors. Just as Henri Matisse turned cut paper into fine art, Butler is taking quilting to new heights.

Butler did not set out to be a quilter when she studied art at Howard University. She was inspired by artists like Loïs Mailou Jones, but she didn't feel truly connected with painting and couldn't use toxic materials around her young child. A textiles class in graduate school was a revelation. She knew how to sew from her mother and grandmother, both dressmakers, and realized this was also a way to express her art.

A portrait to honor her grandmother helped her refine her process: working from an old photograph, she pieced and layered bits of cloth from her grandmother's life. Every fabric choice in a Butler quilt means something—batiks from Nigeria, West African wax prints, Kente cloth from Ghana, where her father was born. Even the fabric's designs add meaning: Frederick Douglass wears a vest adorned with birds symbolizing freedom, while the letters on his sleeves represent his skill with language.

Butler purposely uses an art form trivialized as "women's work," with a long tradition in African American communities, to explore how Black lives and experiences have been undervalued. History-makers like Douglass, pop culture icons like Questlove, or unknown people from vintage photos stand proud and tall, dressed in their Sunday best and gazing back at the viewer with power and dignity. She has quickly become a major force in contemporary art, stirring important conversations about history and injustice.

BISA BUTLER

Born 1973

CITY OF ORANGE, NEW JERSEY (USA)

ICONIC ARTISTS

SALMAN TOOR

The artist who borrows from art history to explore modern identity

Early in his career, Salman Toor made lovely, well-executed paintings in the style of the European Old Masters he had studied for years. He made a living on his talent but felt like he needed to move in a new direction. He turned his technical mastery to more personal subjects, moments based on his life as a gay Pakistani-American man moving between cultures. The power of his new work has turned him into an art world star, with museums all over the world clamoring to show and collect his work.

Toor grew up gay in a very conservative culture. He went to an all-boys school in a country where homosexuality is illegal, but found safety and community in the art room, where he could just be himself. He came to the US to study, and upon moving to New York fell in love with the city's nightlife and accepting atmosphere.

His canvases show everyday scenes of young, queer Brown men going about their lives in the South Asian and North American worlds Toor inhabits. His style is loose and colorful, sketched out in short brushstrokes and often tinted bottle-green or a hazy yellow. He makes visual references to Old Masters like Edgar Degas, Rembrandt, and Johannes Vermeer, but sets them in modern situations.

Like Henri de Toulouse-Lautrec, Toor paints his figures with humanity and empathy, showing tenderness for people often pushed to the margins of society. He explores ideas about race, immigration, and community, both in relaxed private scenes among friends and in public spaces like an airport. At times playful, at times anxious, his intimate portraits challenge stereotypes and make the moments of daily life into fine art.

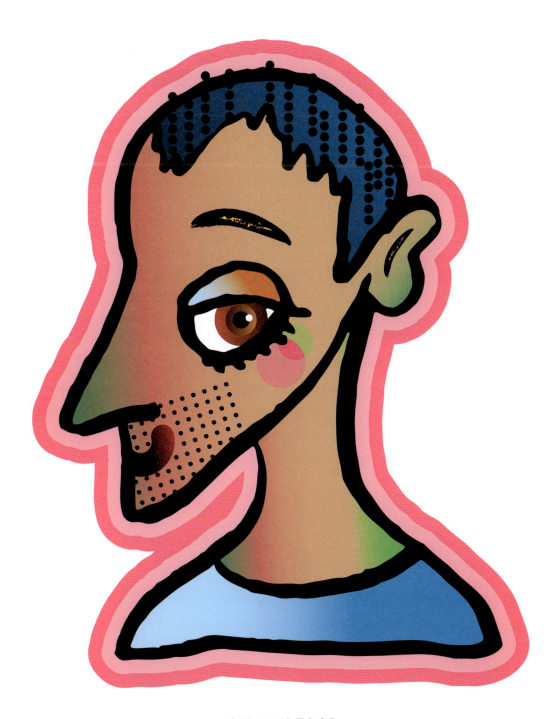

SALMAN TOOR
Born 1983
LAHORE (PAKISTAN)

ICONIC ARTISTS

ICONIC ARTISTS

DAVID LEE CSICSKO is an award-winning artist and designer whose distinctive artwork, stained glass, and mosaics beautify train stations, hospitals, and universities across the Midwest and East Coast. His many credits include designing the Obamas' White House Christmas in 2012. David's lively illustrations can also be seen in *The Skin You Live In* from the Chicago Children's Museum, now in its 16th printing, *LGBTQ+ Icons*, *Science People*, *Iconic Composers*, and *Fashion Icons*, the first four books of the People Series. Through his use of color, bold graphics, and playful patterns, David Lee Csicsko celebrates the richness and diversity of life.

LINDY SINCLAIR has worked in design, music, politics, printing, and publishing, but reading has always been her first love. She is also the author of *Science People*, the second book in Trope's People Series with David Lee Csicsko. She grew up in northeast Ohio but now lives, reads, and knits in Chicago.

ICONIC ARTISTS

© 2024 Trope Industries LLC.

This book and any portion thereof may not be reproduced or used in any manner whatsoever without the express written permission of the publisher. All rights reserved.

© 2024 Illustrations by David Lee Csicsko
© 2024 Text by David Lee Csicsko & Lindy Sinclair

LCCN: 2024937384
ISBN: 978-1-9519632-1-7

Printed and bound in China
First printing, 2024

David Lee Csicsko's illustrations from *Iconic Artists* are available for purchase. For inquiries, go to trope.com or email the gallery at info@trope.com.

+ INFORMATION:
For additional information on our books and prints, visit trope.com

For a glossary of terms referenced in *Iconic Artists*, visit trope.com/iconicartists